Soundtrack

Life is what happens
while the music plays
and we can try to pretend
otherwise – press pause –
try to escape through bad girls,
hot dogs and stuffed monkeys.
But these are just circus fragments,
they do not dispel the tune only
mix in a new arrangement.

Yes, we cannot go back to
the beginning + start over
though we'd sometimes like
to, some wheels were set in
motion a long time ago and I'll
be damned if they'll ever stop...

Circus Fragments

and Other Poems

by Gordon Purkis

Shoe Music Press

Cover Images in the Public Domain courtesy of The Morgue
File www.morguefile.com

Published in Association with Shoe Music Press,
(www.shoemusicpress.com) and Create Space
(www.createspace.com)

The author wants to thank you personally for your purchase
and support of poetry.

Table of Contents

Circus Fragments

Playing War

Thanking the Saints

Circus Fragments

Balloon

I'm beautiful and colorful, but what else?
I live on the edge of death.
I float proud and free, though
I walk on the ledge of despair—
                              my fate sealed.
It takes a whole lot of joy
   to get me up high in the
      sky and keep me there.
I am attracted to static
      and when poked, I pop.

No. 13 on the sideline

He sits on the bench
painted face and surreal,
darkly comical,
jocular but sad and damned—
he is Al Jolson—
and he will continue
to sit humbly, staring down
at the turf, hardly seeing anything
and fumble at another
day.

Genus *Baboon*

Laugh with the man
who calls his cat a monkey,
it exhibiting like behavior, he
forgetting who is the primate.

And he, believed to
be related to apes, laughs
at his own buffoonery, at
not knowing himself all that well.

Antecedent of Death

Contemptuous of life,
he is the man who
rues the onset of the green leaves,
not for their coming,
but for what they will later
become: another year gone by,
another pile of wasted
energy to be gobbled up
in his own fire.

Acrimonious towards time,
he is the man who
wants his work to be finally
done; he doesn't want
another spring because
it only means another autumn,
another packing up and
shuffling off to the colder
layers beyond the reach
of his present certainty.

Here

I will wait for you at the end of the world,
I will see you there,
I will be leaning up against
the wall,
you will be hurried and worried,
standing in line for that
something that never
came, expecting it to come
like a light-switch dawn,
and your cronies will be only
ponies in their stirrups,
baying to be lead away by those
sad straps to chew and sulk,
and I will stop believing in the impossible
tragedies of pure fiction created by my mind,
the cars will stop snaking up the
hill like some bright shiny mindless train
with its light and windows and nothing and
everything will exist just the same but
the in-between-here-and-there will
cease to be and wherever it is you think you
are, wherever it is you think you're headed,
that will all end and you will be here.

End-field

This is where the truncation
of my love began,
on rainy nights, walking
aimlessly in leather
past cold-shouldered cars
but protected by the angels that
watch over true and bad telephone lovers,
who come armed with cupcakes
and sob-story shoulders to cry on.

Sleeping Dragon Motif

I grind my teeth
  and it is like
    my love

I grind my teeth
      and it is persistent
        as relentless
          as it can be

it is abrupt & hard
it is black & fierce
with bright glowing eyes
it is triumphant & true
  hardheaded
      heroic
        & heartfelt

like the uncovering of
treasure that
once belonged to you.

Gordon

I can only be expected
to be, just be, there,
a mound of dirt, roots & rock
& let the animals play upon me
& let the worms crawl through me
& feel the rain fall on me
& see the sun rise and set on me
& accept the living & the dying
& never let science destroy me.

Primitive Genius

I am a monkey
in the shape of
a man.

My suffering is
of my own
design.

My will only
incubates more
indulgence.

Trust that my
only success will
be death.

Local Color

It is a strange romance,
this spinning and shaking
in black leather pants,
everything giggling and flashy,
short skirts and nothing but
leg and fabulous hair a la
Sarah Jessica Parker.

And although my love lies
dashed upon the floor
like a tiresome board game,
its pieces broken and lost,
it is a strange romance with
beer and money, one more piss-pit
dive bar we have made our own.

Fall Equinox

Summer is unlike spilt milk—
it *is* a big deal when you
let it get past you as darkness is
now getting its fill in consuming
our short days.

                And the dogs aren't
as playful and the poets sleep,
you cocoon in your comforter
contemplating coming out again
sometime in spring.

I will implode

My eyes will swell up
    and pop out
of their sockets and bounce
    metallic on the floor
like ball bearings
    and they will skate away
on the linoleum like
    marbles;
great fish will leap from
    my nose and my teeth will
grind, clenched like an
    amputee devotee;
my shoulders will slump
    and cotton candy will issue forth
from my ears like Kleenex
    and my knees will give out
as I crumble under the weight
    of myself,
when the last carnival has
    packed up and gone away
with the little men and horses,
    leaving nothing at all
behind except the pain of finality and
    the uncertainty of another year.

The darkness of not having won

As time rolls over
you like a gang
of thugs,
going high on you and
cutting your legs out low,
you sink deeper into
the realization that
you are already
gone from the here
and now, your efforts
get dragged out to a pale-
green sea, to be swirled into
the nothingness of time until
they no longer resemble anything,
to be hidden from the eyes of the
people crawling all about you,
at your left, at your right, and
at your back, creeping all over
the earth.

As time laps
against your calves
on its way back out,
as you wade into the mild surf,
you stand on tiptoe to look out
over the horizon
to see it go, all your
effort, all your
candescence amid
the darkness of
not having won.

Horse Show

The saddest thing is
when the festival leaves
town and the
tents are taken down by those
shirtless sunburned men in cutoffs
and work gloves, always
waving signals across the field
and the Porto-lets are cleaned out
and loaded on the truck
by always-filthy old men
and taken away.

And instead of staying blissfully
dozing in the carnivalesque
dream, we must stop chasing
love and pleasure, we must awaken
and return to wherever
it is we came from,
                all of us,
sometime / somewhere
no-matter-where-or-when,
to town we must return
from our fanciful
country roamings.

Under the Precarious Sky

I hold my breath in fear,
as to not disturb its quiet

throw. Fetal, covered up,
with nuclear insights.

Dawn seems so fragile and
perfect. There is no motion.

There is only everything
that has been left undone.

Gust

The wind is just whipping,
knocking down signs
and weak children.

Do I really go on this ride?

The power's out, the
whole town seems
evacuated.

Should I be crying?

Macho

I'm a madman
and sane enough
to know it.

It's a circus, an
incredible f'n circus
of pain and snickering
laughter.

And the end will
fall on you like a load of
bricks from a broken
chain on high,
a gigantic elbow
drop from the top rope
and the pinfall
is just three more seconds
of your life you
spent unconscious.

Sadly Serious

You were really more secure as a child
because you were too stupid or naïve
to know you might feel subconscious
as an adult.

So you could easily dress up and play
the part of a semi-glam, semi-starving
artist polo-shirt-with-raised-collar-wearing-
type of sleazy nightclub entertainer at age 8.

You could go on *"Sally's Most Talented
Kids"* and be brought back in serial *ad infinitum*
on re-runs and everyone could say how cute you
were and how adorable yet remarkably profes-
sional though sadly serious.

Circus Fragments

The shirts and pants waving on the line
are like people coming
around the corner,
out of the blind spot of your eye,
from some other reaches of surprise
and you startle a bit,
then realize they have
no arms, no bodies, no legs
and most importantly
no heads but the ones
you choose to put in them.

Playing War

Smeared History

I've written some notes
on vision.
But the art of storytelling is dead.
It died along with things like family picnics
with children in wading pools, old cameras
and the grass is so long.
I don't remember how they used to tie one on.
People who babysat me disappeared.

Sun dried old men who once fought wars
of heroism. Grandpa is tattooed and
has arms that could lift the sky.
I don't seem to see what others do in boxes
of old photos and jars of old foreign money.
Stepping back in time before
I knew any of anything.

Spring in Paris, 1940

Could it have really been all that serious on an un-matched spring day in Paris 1940 when the enemy marched in with perfect grace? I capture moments like these that remind me of you when we were together: so beautiful, yet forceful, sad and ephemeral. Because we were all really there once, to take a foreign love and a simple meal and to breathe the perfect air. But these things of poetry, these butter-cups and moths stirring at dusk hide deep politics: at times I loved you with a fever that crept into a fury like some mad excerpt from Hitler's propaganda machine. And I could say that I intended to liberate you from yourself, to wake you from your languid dream—a warm, contented full-stomached nap. I think on it all, about being there and the larger world outside my own (only more permanent if you allow it), and I still must ask: was it really all that serious when defeat was inevitable? We all know evil never triumphs over good in the end, over the thrushes, ladybugs and swaying meadows. Philosophy never erases the simple sounds of clanking dishes, your feet on the dirt road as you walk home at dusk. I'll never repeat those mistakes: the ones of trying too hard for *decisions*, of taking a lover by forced march with an overpowering occupation army. I intend to visit with my duffel and cigarettes, have a glass of wine with you and your countrymen and go along home and remember you on the way back with butterscotch candy and no further attachments.

Pull

So many people have
pulled on the infectious rope
of crime.

So many cats have
choked on their last rat
where hunger meets death.

So many birds have come
down to Earth to stay
for Sir Isaac Newton.

So many ways to die.
So many ways to kill.
So many ways to go on living.

My Hiding Place

My poetry lies facedown
on the bed, saying
"do not read me."

My best friend Aspirin
takes a night off
from the carousing.

My body searches
for a place to rest
with no floor below,
no ceiling above.

My soul searches for
a forest in which to hide
while my ventriloquist
pen, giving orders to
the gardeners, speaks
from my hiding place.

Playing war

O yeah sure
we played with toys
that snapped and
buzzed and gleamed
with destruction
and we held in our
small fists miniatures
of things that were
pointedly unreal,
winged things, things
with purely plastic souls—
and the music we played:
hatefully loud and fast and
mad about hair, *no more*
teachers no more books, and
as the Reagan years passed
we were all together,
seemingly blissfully
happy still playing war and
deciding outcomes
    that we knew could never happen
      because after all they were
         too good.

It Will Not Have Me

I am positively a
supporter of that
which says that
some-other's noises
are not for caring to
look out at them, through the
shades in the night driveway.

And at any anger
I punch, punch, punch
here at my chest and down to my own gut
and my soul and deeper—

The Guilt of the Living

Watch. Watch as death falls
from the sky in a thousand pieces.
Watch as the fireball consumes
more of our construction. Watch
me, sitting quietly in my corner.
Watch me, saddened with
the guilt of the living. Watch my
calm stare, my mouth open,
my lips do not move.

The Anger of the Truth

I'm only thirty I know
but I will continue to
count the years, make
an addition for a subtraction,
tally up these goings-on,
so many years from start
and ? years from stop.

How is it one thing that grows
decreases my remaining
moments, my very breaths
like a door slowly swinging
shut in contempt of its once
open limitlessness?

And in between we've read
Ethan Frome and been dis-
appointed by so much more
poetics, so many yard sale signs
and beanstalk stories
but not very much poetry
have we found hidden in
these corn rows.

And I've held the
anger of the truth like my wind,
the woefulness of Mr. Shakespeare
reminding me what it is to be
hopelessly mid-card like
Mr. X in a wrestling match.

But the fact that we continue
to fight makes us tougher
than the anger of the truth,
the anger or the truth most
don't stand to face,
tough as hell.

Life story

Everyone's half-hour TV special
dedicated to their memory

begins with black and white
photos of their parents who

grew up in a small town in
Iowa somewhere where the

odds that they'd get away from
the farm and make it big

were a million to one.

And it fast-forwards past all
the years of schooling,

prom dates.

And then you find yourself in the
middle of it all, standing on the

train platform with your blue blazer
with gold buttons with anchors on them

and nobody thought that you'd sing rock n' roll
someday and fly around the world in

murderous planes.

Perspectives

At this distance the crows
That are about to fly by the window
Are the same size as the A-10 that
Was just overhead a moment ago but
Now far gone.

And "the sound of the men working
On the chain gang" clues me back in
To where I am, this perspective
Amongst the suits, sitting eating
Their 6" subs definitely with their
Own chains (we dress up rarely
'Cause we're in business to make
Money, not win a fashion show).

So, it's all really how you look at things;
There are those that are far off that are
Just as near, and those that are near
That are truly far off; birds and planes,
Chains and gangs, subs and suits.

And if they make a sound they go "Ooh-aah."

Odysseus was stuck in traffic

Odysseus was stuck in traffic
on I-84 coming home through
Hartford on his way back
to his Ithaca in the suburbs.

Or he had to stay late at the office
because work was really piling up
but he really had his secretary
on the desk in his office.

Or he just took a shine to traveling
because of the draggings of home
where pretenders await his return
like emboldened mice who feast openly.

He took the scenic route to beat
the traffic crowds and put a little
space between him and the others
who prefer to remain motionless.

But when he finally did get home
he found a way to put it all right
again, tuck the kids in their tidy beds
and kiss good-nite an oblivious wife.

Had he a right to call this home?

Lyrical Aesthete

I will rendezvous with raven-
headed women with blood-
red lips beside mysterious
pools of mercurial water.
Blood-red, as visually shocking
as fresh blood on a
white white shirt.
Red like the only color you
can see in a dream.
My character will be its
own plot device and I will
live on serially in the dreams
of others.
Not a living life, but just
drawn-out death,
sitting in darkness by
shaded gates and talking
slowly and clandestinely,
my eyes glowing
white and watery in the darkness,
my teeth chattering, chi-chi-chattering
as I wait for fortuitous chance in knifelike fear,
crouching below-decks like a stowaway,
spidery and patient.

Winter Pickings

Winter pickings are slim
chances at survival but
the birds keep after it,
pecking at the ground
freshly chilled with a thin
layer of new snow;
squirrels are smart enough
and strong enough
to make holes in screening
to get at the birdseed
that you carelessly left
in plain view;
my mice have plenty of
peanut butter from my
unreliable traps—
they are fat and warm under
the attic insulation and
I almost don't mind it;
buried here under my sheets,
life is so hard and death
so easy, when you can order
it up like fast food, but it
takes something, takes caring
to take care and be calm
while breathing slowly,
holding it in (no exhalation
or reprieve) while calmly
waiting for spring.

Fancy

In my dreams my whitewall
tires
are always bright and
clean
and I have both radio
knobs.
And the hills are higher and
more
rising, like an amusement
park's
Viking battleship: "whoop-see-daisy,
whoa-see-daisy"
almost like falling off the back of a
chair.
And I fancy that like a child's plastic
yacht upon
the bathtub sea, someday we'll
really founder
and all hands will be lost in the
depths of
someplace I can't fathom to say.

Flexing your Muscles

A rattlesnake and a kitty cat play tag
On the kitchen floor, fighting for the
Sole right to wear those rusty stripes
That they share commonly, that are the
Technicolor-orange in those old movies
Of football games back when they wore
Leather helmets.

A crazy spinning ball of reckless color
In an environment so sterile and polished
Like the adds in the 50's with mom selling
Soap and moping the floor in black pumps,
Spouting the virtues of what does wonders
For her linoleum ice rink and "Just look at that
shine!"

Remember to Breathe

I live in the apocalypse of
every moment falling like rain,
passing by like soda bubbles in
time. I die in the revelation of every
morning beginning again like yes-
terday, somewhat forgotten like
history. When you live among the
animals pray, pray for the charisma of
your charm and the strength of
your door lock to hold, see in each
moment the proximate cataclysm that
somehow does not ever happen and
remember to breathe out and in again.

Freshman

A crass crusader for
Anything that surprises,
Flatters, or even kindly
Insults your
"Never would have thought that"
Mind. An eighteen year old blush
As red as the sweater you wear
That shows off your tiny breasts
So well. People watch when you
Walk. You breed with the world
In unconsciousness.
A weed that grows in the muck.

And once you've finally been forced
To thoroughly hate the sex you'll
Drink and dry and say
You've had plenty of the "I love you's"
Of teenage empty-threats.
In solid sculptures your story is told.
Six thousand years of foreplay.

A Midsummer's Night

People, even ferry Goodfellows
seldom get it right the first time

but a Comedy of Love
is my industry

this century the same
as any other

unfolding souls similar,
barring technology.

They did it on foot
on bicycles
in cars

the chase goes on
to wound Dianna

with a man's broad
stroke

as inaccurate Cupid's
arrows fall to earth

to sting a flower
with a name.

Thanking the Saints

A Different Christ

I kind of
wish we had two-
thousand years to
start over,
although you know what
they say: *you learn
from your mistakes*
but enough already,
how many more
times could we let
Charlie kill
and never mind Adolph?

I want a different
Christ, one who
doesn't die on the
cross,
one who
    doesn't demand
the impossible church
and give
me the wrong
tools to build it,
not a carpenter
but perhaps
an enigmatic
        pragmatist
a poet who
works in
cement overtures.

No Savior

You don't walk away
from a house that's
      burning
or a faucet that's running
and
if you consider each leaf
that falls to be an unloved
      soul, you may
want to reach out and
catch at least one
lovingly,
break out of your
fen of hatred
and save something or
someone from
disaster.

But as the cricket
chirps (it does its thing)
you say: leave the wheel-barrowing
to the wheel-barrowers,
it's not my job to
save the world or even
make it that much better—

I mean just
look at what Christ
and Columbus
had to go
through
and see

the shape
of the
world
these days.

Thanking the Saints

Remember the keepsakes and pray to the
Highway gods to help you make good time.

Remembering to thank St. Jude for granting
unspoken petitions of last week in a small three-
town advertising-driven gazette where you can
pick up old records, baseball memorabilia and
used gardening equipment.

I thank the saint of keeping my shit together
like being able to keep all the pens with their caps,
match up all the socks and making sure the rubber
bands, tacks and paper clips don't end up all tan-
gled together in an amorphous, useless ball.

I always save the yellow copy and
remember to retain it for my records.

A votive candle helps big time.

Patting God on the Back

You really should
once in a while
thank somebody for
parting the clouds
just at the right moment,
for the opportunity to
grill chicken
out in the yard
which you took no
part in killing
and for
the whippoorwills
that are scattered everywhere
this time of year
so quite by design.

So take a rainbow—
something good after something
some think bad;
to me rain is an activity at
the very least-and sun is how
California got so lazy.

Take getting to work on time
despite the traffic.
Take going to bed early and
waking up late anyway.
Take impossible contrivances
that work out just fine.

(Continued on page 50)

(Continued from page 49)

Take the old man trimming
shrubs outside your window
with a rag hanging out of
the gas can functioning
in the place of some lost cap.
Take these things and
Take care.
Take them and you'll see that
Paradise was never
really destroyed— it
was just spread out
a little thinner
for all us poor folk.

Smells

Some dumb luck in that response that triggers instant recollections of having been somewhere in time before like smelling elsewhere that fruity shampoo your girlfriend used to wash you out of her hair with and her sweat and those thoughts of the day too, her salty libido released at eventide.

And naked in the sand on the beach you smell that fragrance on the breeze that they've imitated in some colognes, mixed with a moon-driven smell of heat from a werewolf hidden behind a tree in the woods and the smell of your own protective saint that keeps him from killing you.

And although they don't all make it, the sea turtles smell the sea and crawl back towards it.

Open All the Time

I see, I judge. It's these damn eyes—open all the time.

A place...everywhere. Everywhere a place.

I see things there: plants, animals, and people. Always moving, always doing.

But it seems so improbable—all at once so beautiful and so ugly,
like they are hardly there.

Without these eyes, oh lord yes, they would be gone.
Without these eyes—a rather ingenious excuse not to see!

See the football games!
See the disappointed faces!
See the ruinous ends of haughty beginnings!
See chance!
See the sleeping!
See the disturbed!
See their soft forms bouncing through their years!
See madness!
See me!

But I am not so mad to want these things gone.
Not so mad in wishing I could close up and turn off.

Rather, sane enough to know that the tough men
don't quit something that gets at them, they make
the to-do lists,
tie up loose-ends and somehow make it,
running full-blast but always empty,
always hungry for an impossible fuel,
open all the time.

My Yellow

All I know about is today—right now.
Yesterday is dead and tomorrow doesn't
exist but in anticipation. What is the reason
for anticipation? You cannot control what
will happen in your day (today's episode
of your life). O for stopping on reds and
continuing on greens. But safety is yellow,
your yellow. My yellow is my love posing in front
of her yellow convertible, her yellow sweater
reminding me of the fact you do dream in
color and the souls of dead loves live forever.

Memorandum on Your Sky

I could call you up to tell you
"don't worry, your sky is not
falling" and you could believe
me.

Or, if you weren't there, I could
leave you a message on your
voicemail saying "it's just me
calling to say that your sky is
not falling, not falling again."

Hell is Burning

Hell is burning and I don't care,
I know it seems unnecessary to say it
but I'll say it again, hell is burning
and I am here: surrounded by cauldrons
of hot liquor I cannot taste nor drink.

Hell is burning meanwhile the rest
has a slow {tick} or sways like the
palms, rustles or rolls in the breeze.

Hell is burning and I know you know
but they may be baking brownies and
I'm sure you'll want some o' *those*.

Hell is burning and I'm on time
or I'm late (for work or play)
but it doesn't matter and well,
I need some reading light
anyway so let's pretend that you're
fire and I'm wood and let's let our past—
I want to let the past burn like sticks
and never reappear, even as smoke.

Mothers and Fathers

It's a rule that they don't
have funerals or bury
the dead on holy days.

The channel is temporarily
closed down like Union
shops on a holiday.

And your folks stay in or
go out or you really don't
notice and the hours of
daylight are at a premium.

The chalice is raised and
the bread is broken and
all mothers and fathers rest
in peace wherever they lay.

Gone Fishing

It may not be as bad as it seems
but it probably is – so just relax –
think of it in less serious terms of
today, but in more serious terms of
choosing living over dying for tomorrow.
I romanticize the not-so-romantic past so
I may wine and dine the future, thoughtfully
thoughtless about the facts as they often
occur to me during moments when I stand
in the ultimate reality of truth-be-told. How
easily I try to forget the evidence in evidence:
that I've used the wrong tools for the job in
just about every instance, that I've tried death
as an option to life, that I've gone fishing
hoping to catch absolutely nothing.

The Value of Soul

If she loves me I'm sure there's a good reason
and
if she loathes me I'm sure there's a better one: via
her method of divining the value of soul –
a way I haven't thought about – as I stumble
around like some poor blind creature, stuck in the
middle of
someplace
smack-dab in the heart of obscurity
where
I can only feel with my fingers the cool slimy
walls of its
insides and listen and smell for the entrance
or the exit
or wherever it is I can find
escape.

White

Is the color of your twin soul,
the one you are supposed to love
without effort, without denial, without
fear of loss but to her you may be
black or even just red, to be loved
in return in only a purely abstract way,
for the distance between our fingers
is too great at this moment and our
voices do not ever meet for coffee
anymore nor preach to the darkness
for it to give way to light – when
dawn surely comes to rescue us from
our worries, our bad dreams, our past
failures to be one with each other.

Sitting Like a Spider

Sitting like a spider on the basement floor,
patient, awake, but motionless for days
at a time, waiting for that crucial moment
that demands action.

Sold to you stories of lovers torn apart
by violent storms that bring into focus the
active pain of mortal joy, the passion for Being
that makes it all seem worthwhile.

Alive or dead, to have loved and loved
truly is all that matters.
Without having done so, I have no soul, no sense
that existence is greater than all the unimportant
things that rule this waking consciousness.

Sitting like a spider not
seeming to breathe,
watching time pass without
change, without love and
the mortal joy to bait me.

Acknowledgements

"Smeared History" appeared in New Dimensions 1997. ECSU Press.

"Spring in Paris, 1940" from Poet's Corner October 1998 Vol. 2 #14

"Playing War" appears on Rogue Scholars (www.roguescholars.com)

"The Anger of the Truth" appears in *the eye #3 December 2005*

"Life Story" appears in New Works Review (online-defunct)

"Perspectives" online in the Red River Review # 56 (www.redriverreview.com)

"Odysseus was Stuck in Traffic" online in Pif #30, November 1999 (www.pifmagazine.com)

"The value of Soul" appears in # 38 and **"Gone Fishing"** in #37 of Zygote in My Coffee (www.zygoteinmycoffee.com)

"Hell is Burning" "A Different Christ" and **"My Yellow"** are found in the *Tribal Soul Kitchen* (www.tribalsoulkitchen.com)

"No Savior" appears in *The Kings English* (www.thekingsenglish.com) 2004

"Remember to Breathe" "Here" "Lyrical Aes-
thete" "Open All the Time" "Antecedent of
Death" "The Guilt of the Living" "Winter Pick-
ings" and "Fancy" all appear at
www.alittepoetry.com

"White" can be found in *Word Riot*
(www.wordriot.org)

"Patting God on the Back" appeared in *Ancient
Paths* Issue 9 Fall 2002

"Mothers and Fathers" "Sadly Serious" and
Sitting Like a Spider" appeared in *Wired Hearts*
(online-defunct)

www.ingramcontent.com/pod-product-compliance
Lightning Source LLC
Chambersburg PA
CBHW060424050426
42449CB00009B/2113